Five Addled Etchers

The first Hamilton B. Mitchell Lecture

on Printing and Graphic Arts

FIVE ADDLED ETCHERS by
LEONARD BASKIN

DARTMOUTH PUBLICATIONS
HANOVER · NEW HAMPSHIRE

for Lisa

Illustrations

I Duvet. St. John Writing The Apocalypse.

II Duvet. St. Michael and the Dragon. The Apocalypse.

III Duvet. St. Peter and Moses.

IV Duvet. St. Andrew, St. Roch and St. Sebastian.

V Seghers. Landscape with Waterfall.

VI Seghers. Rocky River—Landscape with Highroad.

VII Seghers. Tempest.

VIII Seghers. Bemossed Tannenbaum.

IX Seghers. Two Trees.

X Seghers. Great Tree.

XI Vellert. Vision of St. Bernard.

XII Vellert. St. Luke Painting the Virgin.

XIII Vellert. Temptation of Our Lord.

XIV Meryon. The Morgue.

XV Meryon. Le Ministère de la marine.

XVI Bresdin. The Good Samaritan.

Even from the depths of Hell his voice I hear
Within the unfathomed caverns of my ear.

BLAKE

Addled, tonight, is meant to mean hallucinated. Our 'addled five' diverge from the mien and stance of other etchers, in that where others are free, even frolicsome, they are tight, even constricted. Instead of being spontaneous, a prime characteristic of etching, they will be labored, studied, contrived and crabbèd. Each suffers from the horror of vacant spaces, and each tends to inform the common with aspects of the wondrous. Objects, noble and mundane, pure and simple, are transmogrified, metamorphosed, and folded to enchantment. Lemurs and monkeys haunt their religious landscapes. Demons annex the air of their government buildings. Plain fields are made rough, and figures in their apocalypse scenes jostle one another. Their St. Luke is myopic, and like themselves hallucinated. They are in fact divine deviants. Their names: Jehan Duvet, Hercules Seghers, Dirck Vellert, Charles Meryon and Rodolphe Bresdin.

Jehan Duvet

UNTIL virtually yesterday, Duvet's genius has been the object of scorn and calumny. Even Hind, who does see in Duvet a kinship with Blake, writes in the 1908 edition of his *A Short History of Engraving and Etching*: 'He never mastered the elements of drawing and never got beyond a heavy and overcharged manner of engraving, in which an irregular shading is outlined with thick strokes often carelessly doubled and doubled again.' An earlier biographer of Duvet is deprecatory rather in the manner of Dr. Thornton, who made clear to his readers, in one of the great chicken-hearted notes of all time, that Blake had more of genius than of art. The dates of Duvet's birth and death, the chronology of his works, are all still in doubt. Those ornaments of pedantry need not, I trust, worry us unduly. That Duvet was born circa 1485 in the surroundings of Dijon is accepted. He was a goldsmith participating

13

Duvet in the fêtes attending the entry into Langres of François I, preparing the jeweled bowl that was presented to the king. There is great Italianate influence in the engraved work of Duvet, although that influence was from the first fiercely joined in the style which was inimitably his. Mantegna, whose entombment he copies, was the principal source, and to a lesser extent Raphael via the medium of Marcantonio's engravings.

Duvet's works are peopled with a great and festooned horde, tumbling and flying, gyrating and gesticulating with wild abandon. Unyielding in the delight of his excess, he covers every plate with the fancies of his vision. A. E. Popham's splendid phrase, 'grotesque intensity,' is perfect in its evocation of the carroling grandeur of his 'Apocalypse.' Many of the apocalypse plates derive directly from Dürer. But where Dürer is clear and meditative, Duvet is artfully confused and impassioned. Dürer provides a kind of visual nomenclature for the vision of John. Duvet enchants that mystery with the wonderment and quasi-reality of visionary chaos, and invests Dürer's nomenclature with the spasms, gasps, and ecstasy of revelation. There is an insatiable madness to capture every detail of the thunderous glory of St. John's vision. The work was published in 1561. It was printed by Jean de Tournes, the great typographic genius of Lyons, and only five copies of the book survive. Duvet had been called 'le maître à la Licorne' because of an allegorical series dealing with the amours of Henry II and Diane de Poitiers. The allegory has never been clearly explicated: Diane, the king, and the unicorn figure rather bewilderingly as the chief actors. Unicorns are captured only with the pure involvement of an

14

FATA PREMVT
TREPIDANTQS
MANVSIAM
LVMINA EALVAT
MEVS RESTAT
VICTRIXGRA
DEQ SVADET
OPVS

SACRA IN HAC ET ALIIS SEQVĒTIBVS
TABELLIS CONTENTA MISTERIA EX
DIVINA IOHANNIS APOCALIPSI DESVPTA
SVNT AC VERÆ LITERÆ TEXTVS
PROXIME ACCOMMODATA ADHIBITO
ETIAM VIRORVM PERITIORVM IVDICIO

unsmutched virginal lass. In one of the plates, the unicorn rests his head in the worn lap of the moon goddess, Henry's middle-aged mistress. A profuse, buffoonish piece of flattery. Mantegna's monumental, anguished, awesome, seminal, wondrous print, 'The Entombment,' transcribed and reversed by Duvet is recognizably Mantegna's, but O how strange, and how wild! Thus the gesticulating figure is become more frantic, more uncontrolled in the stance of yelping misery. This is a great characteristic of Duvet: he looses his passion totally, no restraint, in seeking to express the inmost heart of his thought and feelings. We read him clear, for this *expressionist* habit is within our ken.

Duvet's greatest work is his 'Apocalypse.' In his crypto-title to the series, the opening plate, the figure of St. John at the table writing is a presumed self-portrait. We begin, here, to see the characteristic style and manner of Duvet. A tumultuous vision begets confusion, but a confusion of spectral order. The apocalyptic plates grow wilder and wilder until one is caught up in the vortex of revelation. Consider this fantasy landscape. A bosky dell, emitting a devil and angel, partially screens a magical city castellated and bespired, fronting on a harbor in which barks of various size mingle, here ordinary fishermen, and just there an immense crescent craft, a ship of state, a fateful poop-deck where the three weird sisters decide the thread-length of our life, and birds, foliage, great cats, and the whole a flashing illumination of the threshold of visionary inquest. Duvet is massively inspired by the Apocalypse of Dürer. Consider the Dürer. The awesome scene of Judgement Day is powerfully and cogently set forth. I sense Pirckheimer beating at

Duvet

PLATE I

17

11 Duvet. St. Michael and the Dragon. The Apocalypse.

Duvet

PLATE II

Dürer's back to insure a stately measure of order and a justness to the text. But Duvet coats Dürer's dry bones with the glaring fervor of that day. Where Dürer is spare, Duvet invests the scene with chaos and the bewildering blinding fulgence of his genius. Duvet's *horror vacui*, a presumed fault, is a golden enrichment. The holy martyrs are here, separate and kept pure by a burning shield, and the recent dead (I knew that Duvet would take macabre delight in detailing the long fingernails and still growing hair of the new dead). Duvet's signature is framed within the tablets of the Law, surely to signify the divine relevance of this work. Again in 'The Angel sounding the sixth trumpet' the tempestuous tumult of tossing and turning figures, gyrating to an overwhelming, celestial jostling. This masterwork is an edifice of hallucinatory glory. A short aside on visionary artists. One observes the faces of Duvet's figures are blank, a great stony open expressionless blankness. In his print

PLATE III

'St. Peter and Moses,' the holy men stare past each other; their great eyes see nothing, but gaze backward, deep into the serried layers of their brains. This is true of Blake and other visionary artists. The expressive phantasmagoria in which these artists delight is never facial but rather in the posture of the body and the charged ambiance. Duvet is expressive in how a figure opens his hand or closes it, in the *bizarrerie* of stance and manner. It is as though he had never heard of Theophrastus.

In his portrayal of the three *good* saints, St. Andrew, St. Roch,

PLATE IV

St. Sebastian (derived in part from Mantegna's 'Risen Christ between St. Andrew and St. Longinus'), who in Christian humility tended the sick and the poor, we find Duvet somewhat less rav-

18

III Duvet. St. Peter and Moses.

IV Duvet. St. Andrew, St. Roch and St. Sebastian.

aged by his obsessional need to *mille-feuille* the plate. But even in this rational depiction, that forest is surprisingly growing out of nowhere and ascending to nowhere. Jehan Duvet, I dare say, was addled; and addled enough for his prints to compel us to intimate gleanings and long and beneficent investigation.

Hercules Seghers

Samuel Hoogstraten, Rembrandt's pupil, tells the life of Seghers as he knows it. He knows, alas, nothing, nor do we, of this lowlander infatuated with alpine fantasies of rock-strewn mountainous building-up valleys that never were. He was born in Haarlem about 1590; studied with Conixloo; and became a member of the Guild of St. Luke in 1612, an *annus mirabilis* for Dutch art. The sordid tale that Hoogstraten tells recounts Seghers's inability to sell his work, his using-up of all the linen in the house for painting and printing, and of mounting debts. Seghers turned to drink and died from a fall in his house. He was a unique and isolated phenomenon in his day and so he remains. The timeless quality of his work, its incisive implications for our time are without parallel. Although it is hardly an encomium, many of his etchings might have been produced in this decade, in the so-called renascence of printmaking.

Seghers

The technical wizardry and innovations of Seghers's prints astound us; and this ingenuity is wedded to a content which called it forth. The subjects of his etchings are, for the greatest part, views of rocky valleys and mountains, tempests at sea, ruins and trees. But the content of these etchings reveals the coruscated facets of his near-demented vision. Such mountains never were. They tower, built of a tumult of rocks, corrugating ever upward. The line sputters and spatters and traverses the entire landscape until it seems alive, a great multi-tiered creature, host to a million maggots, all writhing. A nasty sounding image but somehow expressive of the reticulative surface of his world.

PLATE V

PLATE VI

PLATE VII

The landscape etchings vary greatly in size. Several are large indeed for the Dutch seventeenth century. A world in small opens to our sight. The smooth places made rough, for plains, meadows, and fields there are trenches, gorges, ravines, an earth falling away from heaving mountains all gutted, pitted, rutted, and furrowed: lunary. The landscapes invaded by mists and vapors gloom and enthrall the exhumed land. His tempests are of enormous seas at night wherein a small boat is trapped and inevitably doomed. The etchings of tempests are perhaps the most miraculous and mysterious of Seghers's prints. He made but two, or only two have survived. One is all of brown, the other dense black and black-green. These are night scenes. The sea all aswirl, humped wave upon wave, engulfing the tiny, fitful vessels in a maelstrom of deadly green sea and black night. The sea, the ghastly swollen sea ripping man and his ships. And all of these prints are in color; incredible color. The trees of Seghers push through the earth, generated from

24

VII Seghers. Tempest.

VIII Seghers. Bemossed Tannenbaum.

a magical fuse. One of a great larch inhabits an air all vibrant with a 'Seghers belt' of radiated colors, rose-imbued blues, and green-haunted rose. And the larch itself, or as the German title has it, 'Bemossed tannenbaum,' is asquirm with astonished life. Limbs and boughs lift and fall in every direction, the strands of Spanish moss trailing limp rigging on a ship, vacant and lost. The tree stands enchanted, the emanation of a far-eastern artist alone in a mountaintop studio. Inexplicably it is the work of a Dutchman, a Dutchman touched with the visionary balm.

Two other tree prints of Seghers compel our notice: One of two trees is reminiscent of a Leonardo drawing. The trees are printed in brown on a prepared surface of green-blue-rose. They are ineffably graceful. The space between the two trees is charged, alive with the invisible lines of harmony that play from one tree to the other. The trees do not exist in a given landscape, they co-inhabit the empty field of the print. Here is a felicitous symbiosis. The large etching called 'The Great Tree' is an example of Seghers's technical wizardry. No clear indication of how the white on gray and black has been achieved. The great tree looming over the surrounding trees and buildings seems in bloom, but alas, so do the other trees, bushes, and buildings in the print. There is a towering sense of unreality unfolding here. The great wondrous tree is sick, as is the ambiance and all in it. What was Seghers's intention?

Seghers's method was as follows: He would tint or paint paper or linen with one or more colors and print his etching, usually in a deeper tone of the background color, and elaborate the color further after printing, by painting it again. Plain enough. But Seghers fur-

Seghers

PLATE VIII

PLATE IX

PLATE X

29

Seghers　　　ther compounded the effect by several devices which are still not clear. He had a way of printing in reverse, so that the quality of a negative is achieved. It is not just a question of printing the etching as though it were a relief print, for bizarre intermediate tones are evident. And he scraped the plate to achieve a kind of aquatinting and often crosshatched areas and printed these areas un-inked. Here is technical brilliance spurred by the demands of a necessity bred in Blake's *'unfathomed caverns.'* No one, evidently, wanted these prints, and they are, today, the rarest of all printed images. Rembrandt owned seven of Seghers's paintings and the copperplate of his 'Tobias and the Angel' derived from Elsheimer through the engraving by Goudt. Rembrandt despoiled Seghers's etching by scraping out 'Tobias and the Angel 'and substituting a 'Flight into Egypt' of his own. It's to his credit that he only slightly altered the landscape. Seghers's etchings can be properly seen only at the print cabinet of the Rijksmuseum.

IX Seghers. Two Trees.

Dirck Vellert

UNLIKE Lucas van Leyden, who was his mentor and who probably taught him what our unsullied elders were pleased to call in a quasi-technical way 'process,' unlike Lucas, I say, there are no reworked or exhausted impressions from the plates etched and engraved by Dirck Vellert, who was received into the Antwerp Guild in 1511, and became Dean in 1518 and again in 1526. He entertained Dürer at dinner on the 12th of May, 1521. I think bizarre thoughts about that dinner. The great and mighty Dürer, his Netherlandish journey a triumph, welcomed with awe and reverence everywhere, selling tons of his prints, sits down to dinner with Vellert, who made his living painting glass; or so I imagined it. In fact, Vellert gave a 'costly banquet' for Dürer, inviting many of Antwerp's leading painters and goldsmiths. In January of the same year, 1521, Dürer gave Vellert a set of his Apocalypse and the Six Knots, which were cut in wood after Leonardo's designs.

35

Vellert   Here then is a 'little master' who painted glass but who was sufficiently driven to engrave some twenty odd plates—and rather odd they are. Not absolutely weird, or frenzied or frantically compulsive—but yet not quite wholly sane and 'healthy.' There is an unsettling quality in these plates. Is it the sly archaizing, the sudden stiffening in the mellifluous field? Vellert is a Gothic mannerist. The figures may disport themselves in their serpentine ways, but they are ill at ease, sensing somehow that their gestures hardly conform to their character. The air is sodden and heavy in these prints. They are disquieting.

In dealing with the totality of an artist's work, art historians are at the greatest pains to establish a chronology for the paintings, sculpture, or prints. They deeply investigate style and changes however subtle in that style, subjects related to specific, datable historical events, the sudden appearance of a new influence and sources and various clever and imaginative devices. There is much straining and more disquisition to support and justify a particular dating. Vellert is, I may say, unique in that he gives in unequivocating fashion, the day, month, and year, in all of his prints save three, two have the year and one is undated and unsigned, wherefore I suspect the print as not being by Vellert. What impelled him to consistently add the ephemeral day and month? If his production were prodigal and works poured from him as they do from Picasso, who, when the inspired heat is upon him, does completely date each work—but Vellert's graphic oeuvre is twenty-one prints. They form in their totality a thin fardel of obscurity; obscure to all but those who pick deeply into the wondrous enormity of *graphica* bequeathed

36

XI Vellert. Vision of St. Bernard.

XII Vellert. St. Luke Painting the Virgin.

XIII Vellert. Temptation of Our Lord.

to us. Vellert is not quite addled, but surely odd in his love of days, months, and years. I have noted what I call his Gothic mannerism. That quality is perceived in one of his major prints, the 'Vision of St. Bernard.' Vellert becomes more decidedly addled in his continuous coupling of wildly disparate elements. The very intense Saint Bernard (the daemonic spur of the Second Crusade) and the Virgin are habited in Gothicising robes, angular and sharp, complex and involuted, infolding and overlapping. They inhabit space in front of a great arch resplendent with archaic-like decoration. Panels of ornament festoon the face of the arch. Putti stand and squat above displaying Roman-like standards engraved with the words, Christ and Mary. These names are repeated again on the two panels, above two rondels of helmeted centurions. Great garlands hang in the arch, and two wreaths hang from the garlands. The extreme piety of the scene is made all the more strange for the Virgin sits on a marble bench with satyr heads and legs at its corners. And through the arch is visible a late medieval dorf. The print is signed and dated Oct. 3, 1524. These curious juxtapositions occur in Vellert's larger prints, the wonderful nearsighted 'St. Luke Painting the Virgin'; the 'Temptation of Our Lord,' in which the devil is sporting a very pious look and a pair of slippers anachronistically medieval in the company of the serpentine Christ, serpentine in movement, that is. Is Vellert kin to our addlepated fraternity? Room must be found for an artist who seats a beatific Virgin Mother on a Bacchic bench.

Vellert

PLATE XI

PLATE XII

PLATE XIII

41

Charles Meryon

EVEN the dimmest academician, feverish in his misunderstood adulation of Meryon, sensed that element of dread and foreboding that floats off like a malevolent spirit from the surface of Meryon's prints. From Meryon is dependent a befuddled horde who have aped his telescopic-lens-like vision of buildings, streets, and prospects, but who are utterly innocent of the wonderful dementia that bathed his prints in a spectral glow. Their names are 'illustriously unknown.' Charles Meryon was the illegitimate issue of a prim but amorous English doctor and a slightly deranged French ballet dancer. He was born in 1821. In 1837 he entered the naval college at Brest, evidently was commissioned and made a trip as an officer to New Zealand and Oceania. He was later to do a series of plates inspired by his observations on that trip. Being a marine officer fatigued him, for in a letter he said he was 'not physically or mentally strong

Meryon

enough to be a commander of men' and decided instead on the much more arduous course of becoming a painter, when he discovered to his increasing distress that he was colorblind.

Meryon then turned to etching and never strayed into color except in several etched borders which he printed in a wry orange-red. He acquired the skills of etching from a now thankfully mute practitioner who set him copying etchings of Salvatore Rosa, Karel du Jardin, and Zeeman. He etched in fact eight plates after Zeeman and was deeply affected by the limpid incisive purity of Zeeman's etchings. But the lambent radiance in Meryon's etchings he learned from no one. But he did dedicate his chief work, the 'Eaufortes sur Paris' to Zeeman. Meryon issued his series on Paris between 1852 and 1854 in three parts. Baudelaire spoke of the 'philosophic reveries' in the plates and indeed in 1860 the printer Delâtre invited Baudelaire to prepare a text to accompany the plates. But Meryon resisted the incursion of another's spirit; his mind was filled with verses enough, some of which he etched onto the plates. Meryon's Paris is morbid. The greatest plate of the series, 'The Morgue,' is foreboding, even horrifying; and yet the means used are akin to the invisible terror of Kafka. There is a horror caught in the brilliant sun cutting chasms of blackest death. The alternating densities of black and white, the horrible steaming chimneys (what are they boiling, frying, cooking, burning, in that morgue?). The excavation of space, the deep drops, the great empty frontal plane, the leapings in and out of space, sun, shadow, light, and dark. The upright standing buildings, the windows cerberus-eyed, unblinking, yet alive, more encompassing and all-swallowing like dank and

PLATE XIV

44

LA MORGUE.
1850.

XIV Meryon. The Morgue.

XV   Meryon. Le Ministère de la marine.

rotten caves stained black even in blinding sun. And this sceno-
graphic drop for the *tableau vivant* of suicide, despair, and the
irritating nonchalance of the onlookers, amused, perhaps, as they
gaze from on high, and the *commedia dell' arte* constable pointing
to the tomb. The print has all the dismal horror of Paris; the jeweled chamber of Sainte Chapelle is a dim memory when faced with
this daytime exposé. And how is it achieved? Simple, straight-
forward etching, but heightened by a near insane exactitude. The
unnatural eye, the vision of a triple-eyed cyclops, penetrate the
sinew of stone, the patina of slime, the exact tonality of sun-baked
stucco. And the whole is cast into a sun-beaten terror. Meryon's
claim of insufficient 'mental and physical strength to command men'
would surely extend to the great strain entailed while engaged on
such a piece of work as 'The Morgue.'

And indeed, the growing symptoms of paranoid tendencies, of
which Meryon had given increasing evidence, at last overwhelmed
him and in 1858 he was incarcerated in the insane asylum at Charenton. I should add at this point that the 'Eaufortes sur Paris' received but a dim reception from all but a few who were capable of
discernment. Meryon was reduced to such abject penury that he
was unable to produce the ten sous the printer required for two
impressions of the most beautiful of all his plates, the celebrated
'Abside de Notre Dame.' At the asylum, the charity of sufficient
food, proper lodgings, and a lack of interest in his etchings, slowly
enabled Meryon to achieve a degree of quiet. He was released and
soon his perplexed mind and sane hand were at work producing
new enchantments. Amongst these latter works I will choose only

Meryon

47

Meryon

PLATE XV

one to discuss, the etching called 'Le Ministère de la marine,' which he etched in 1865. In all aspects save one, the stout building which houses this ministry is readily and normally perceived, except that its massive portico and columns are being attacked by a Bosch-like company of demons, devils, warriors astride giant fish, bizarre serpent-like cannon; indeed it is a confraternity doing such battle as has never before been seen. The wonder here is the juxtaposition of the bureaucratic fortress made palpably real by Meryon's near-photographic delineation and the incredulity of a fantasy army swooping down from the skies to attack it. Charles Meryon was reinterned at Charenton in 1866 and died there in 1868. His funeral was attended by Bracquemond, Delâtre, and Philippe Burty.

Rodolphe Bresdin

Bresdin, who was born in 1822, moved in an enchanted trance, was hallucinated with a vision of a world in continual minute eruption, made prints so compulsively dense, so charged with endless minutiae, so peopled with phantoms that the seen and the unseen make a continuous graphic dialectic; and he saw 'the universe in a grain of sand' and beheld all wonder in 'the heavens of hollow flowers.' Bresdin knew and studied the work of earlier artists. No artist, however startlingly original and novel his work, unless he is a primitive, can be without influence from earlier work. Indeed Bresdin looked deeply and was artistically nourished by Altdorfer, Dürer, Ostade, and Rembrandt. Our knowledge of his being influenced by these masters does not diminish our perception of his remarkable transmuting of those older notions by means of his unique sensibility into a vision so personal as to be Bresdin's alone.

49

Bresdin

It is difficult and beyond meaning to graph chronologically his life and movements. He was obsessed with Fenimore Cooper and sought the great virgin forest, even in America and Canada. He came to North America after winning a competition for a banknote design. He was called by some Chien-Caillou (a misreading of Chingachgook of *The Last of the Mohicans*) and by others Le Maître au Lapin, because of a pet rabbit named Petiot who shared a hovel with him in Toulouse, and whom he often carried on his arm. Bresdin was the master of Redon, who signed his first prints, 'élève de Bresdin.' Redon portrayed Bresdin as 'le liseur' in a very beautiful lithograph, and wrote meaningfully and gently of him. The surprising feature of Bresdin's works, beyond its astonishments, is that they contain themselves as works of art. Bresdin's horror of vacant spaces was extreme. He covered the entire surface of each print with a bewildering network of dots and specks, small sharp lines which build in a frenzy of minute growths to ever larger forms until blank space has been driven off. And yet, the work functions as all works of art must as a perceivable, a seeable whole: the work is not fractured into discrete parts. And if we examine his capital work, 'The Good Samaritan,' a fabled spectacle unfolds. In the low center of this large lithograph, 22″ x 17″, a remarkable size for Bresdin, stands the camel, the focal point of the print; he stands all aglow and shimmered in light, caparisoned with Oriental trappings and around him builds a vast fortress of jungle and forest; an opening to the right of the camel gives on a vision of mountains and valleys in which an army swarms, a river opens to a panorama of the holy city Jerusalem. The forests in Bresdin's hallucinated brain

PLATE XVI

50

were inhabited with branches become lizards and demons. On every limb sits a crow, in every crotch an owl; a rat runs along boughs; knots assume a fearful aspect. And everywhere an excrescence of foliage from which peer, as the forest replaces itself into jungle, monkeys and lemurs, marmosets and stranger beasts. A marsh seeps from the jungle at the base of the print, and in it a myriad of birds disport, a great heron, pheasants, and smaller birds of all sorts; and inexplicably a dog breaks from the sedge and drinks. The sky is hung with cloud upon cloud; and into the upper air pushes a great tree, lacy and minutely described. One can never see this print in its total complexity; but in endless searching, in examining it again and again one discovers in the arcane darks of it, new forms and wonders. The figure of the good Samaritan and the object of his charity are naively drawn. Bresdin happily was never properly trained in an academic way and as a result always had great difficulty in drawing the human figure with ease or convincingly. He tends to costume his figures elaborately, usually as Orientals. There are those who think that Bresdin could not have achieved the incredible detail using the fatty grease of the lithographer. They think that Bresdin etched this plate and transferred a wet impression of the etching onto a lithographic stone, and continued working. There is a Bresdin print which exists virtually alike in etched and lithographed form. They may be right. Redon in his writings on Bresdin tells of a flask in which Bresdin kept his liquid grease, and describes how anxious was Bresdin to prevent a speck of dust from marring the fluid. It is quite possible that Bresdin had developed a vehicle with a small quantity of grease to allow for his minute dots

Bresdin

51

Bresdin   and strokes. It must be seen that Bresdin scraped and scraped the stone with a fine metal point quite as much as he drew on it. Since no impression of an etched 'Good Samaritan' has survived, one must assume the existence of the 'marvellous fluid,' which would be in accord with Bresdin's vision and way of working. Bresdin made a great many prints. The exact number is not known. A catalogue raisonné of his graphic oeuvre is in preparation now. That he had no followers is understandable, for Bresdin looked upon the commonplace and saw the miraculous.

XVI Bresdin. The Good Samaritan.

The publishers acknowledge the assistance of the Boston Museum of Fine Arts (plates I, II, IV, XII); The Beinecke Library, Yale University (plates V, VI, VII, VIII, IX, X, XI); the Davison Art Center, Wesleyan University (plates XIV, XV, XVI); Professor Colin Eisler, the Institute of Fine Arts, New York University (plate III); with models for the illustrations in this book.

This book has been planned and supervised by Ray Nash and
printed at The Stinehour Press, Lunenburg, Vermont
Illustrations by The Meriden Gravure Company
Meriden, Connecticut